CW01678371

£4.25

Gary John Lee

CONTENTS

Edited by Michael Stuart Phipps

Contributors: David Boyle, Stuart Branch, John Burns, Louise Cassell, County Studios, Gary Gilbert and Marina Graham.

FIREMAN SAM™ Annual 1991 is published by MARVEL COMICS LTD., in association with THE REDAN COMPANY, 13/15 Arundel Street, London WC2.

Printed in Italy.

FIREMAN SAM

The Talent Contest

This is Pontypandy, a little village that rests somewhere deep in the pretty hillsides of Wales. Fireman Sam lives here. Sam works at the Pontypandy Fire Station.

The fire station is built on a hill overlooking the village. There is a cafe in the village owned by Bella Lasagne. Dilys Price runs Price's General Store.

One day, Sam was working at the fire station. He was busy washing Jupiter, the big, red fire engine. Sam was whistling happily. He *loved* being a fireman.

Station Officer Steele is in charge of the station. "Well done, Fireman Sam!" he said. "Don't forget the talent contest we're holding at the station this afternoon."

Elvis Cridlington is the third member of the fire brigade. "I'm entering as a rock singer!" he said. Sam laughed. "You've got rocks in your head," he said.

The firemen had built a special stage. That afternoon, everyone arrived at the fire station. Bella Lasagne went on to the stage first. "I shall sing-a opera," she said.

"Tra-la," sang Bella, very loudly. Norman Price stuck his fingers in his ears. "*Cor!* What a racket," he grumbled. Bella sang so high, Norman's glasses cracked!

Dilys and Norman Price were going to do a magic trick next. "With the help of my Norman and this hat, I shall make an egg disappear," said Dilys, grandly.

Norman couldn't see properly, because of his cracked glasses. He should have put the hat on Dily's head. Instead, he put the egg on. There was a loud *splaaat*!

"Wait until I get you home, Norman," grumbled Dilys, grabbing him by the ear. It was Trevor Evan's turn next, riding a unicycle. "Bit tricky this," he said

Suddenly, he rode off the stage and landed on top of Station Officer Steele. "*Oof*! I would have expected better of an auxiliary fireman, Evans," said Steele sternly.

Elvis Cridlington ran on stage. "*Ooooh, baby!* Don't give me soup in a bowl, just gim'me rock 'n' roll!" he sang. Norman threw rotten tomatoes at him!

"Your go next," Sam told his nephew and niece, Sarah and James. The children did a series of acrobatics. "*Mama-mia!*" cheered Bella. Then it was Sam's turn.

He wheeled a strange looking machine on to the stage. "This is my latest invention," he said proudly. "A robot that dances and jiggles to its own music!" "*Wow*!" shouted everyone.

Sam pressed the 'on' button. The robot began to play some music, then break-danced on the stage. Then the robot choked and spluttered and started to chase Sam.

"*Great Fires of London*!" cried Sam. "It's out of control!" The robot began tearing down the stage curtains. "*Action stations, Fireman Sam*!" ordered Steele.

Sam borrowed Dily's wand and managed to press the 'off' button. The robot stopped moving. "*Phew!* I really brought the curtains down that time!" laughed Sam.

Sam came last in the talent contest. "Better luck next time, Uncle Sam," said the twins, who had won. Sam blushed. "I think I'll stick to being a fireman!" he chuckled.

The End

Clumsy Cridlington!

Uh oh, and Great Fires of London! Elvis is trying to cook. And as usual, a number of things have gone wrong again! Can you spot the twenty things in this picture that are wrong or out of place?

OIL

A Report!

Hello, readers!

Goodness! What a day it's been! What with the fire at Price's General Store, and rescuing Trevor, I haven't had five minutes to put my feet up!

Luckily, it all turned out well in the end. But as to how it started, well . . .

Dilys Price was feeling very excited. She had invited Trevor Evans over for dinner. Our Trevor is fond of Dilys, so he said 'yes' before she had even finished asking him!

"I'll be over at six o'clock, Dilys," he told her, after buying a bag of jelly babies to eat while he was driving his bus.

"Glad to hear that, Trevor," said Dilys, happily. "I'll cook you something really special! And I'll make sure my little darling is out of the way too!"

Of course, Dilys was talking about her son, Norman. And Norman had overheard her!

"*Heh*! I know!" he chuckled. "I'll play a trick on my Mam! It'll be *ever* so funny!"

Do you know what that rascal did? He swapped the bar of soap in the bathroom for a bar of trick soap from his box of jokes!

"Wait until Mam gets washed!" giggled Norman, going outside to play. "She'll have such a *surprise*!"

Meanwhile, Trevor was paying a visit to the Pontypandy Fire Station. He was pleased to see me in the kitchen, cooking a meal.

He told me about his dinner date with Dilys.

"Funny, that," I said. "I've invited the twins around the station for a meal too. That's why I'm up to my elbows in vegetables!"

"*Hmmm*! Smells good!" said Trevor, having a sniff of the pie I was making.

Trevor left me, hard at work, while he drove his bus around Pontypandy, looking for passengers. He was feeling very nervous and excited about having dinner with Dilys.

"I won't forget this evening in a hurry," he chuckled to himself. And he was right too!

At five o'clock, Dilys decided to close the shop early, to give herself time to get ready for Trevor. She had already put a pan of curry on the gas ring to cook.

"*Ooooh*! That Trevor! He likes his curry," she twittered, as she went upstairs to wash and change.

Norman was waiting in his bedroom. When he saw his mum, he started giggling.

"Ahh, such a happy boy, my Norman," said Dilys, giving his cheek a friendly pinch. "Just make sure you keep out of the way this evening, mind you. I don't want more frogs in my teapot again!"

"Oh, you won't get that, Mam," said Norman, smiling.

Dilys went into the bathroom and started to wash her face with the soap. Suddenly she let out a terrifying, ear-piercing *"Shrrriiiiiiiiieeeeek*!"

She ran out of the bathroom, all of a tizzy. Her face and hands were covered in black ink from Norman's trick soap!

"*Heh, heh!* You do look funny, Mam!" giggled Norman, ducking quickly to miss getting a well-deserved clip round the ear from a very cross Dilys.

"*Ooooh*! You bloomin' nuisance!" cried Dilys, chasing Norman down the stairs and out of the shop. "Wait until I get my hands on *you*! Whatever will Trevor say when he sees me like this?"

Dilys was so busy trying to catch Norman that she completely forgot about the curry cooking on the gas ring. The pan grew hotter and hotter. Thick black smoke began to fill Dilys' kitchen.

Trevor was also having problems. He had been driving along Pontypandy Lane in his bus, when a stray dog ran out in front of him. Trevor had swerved to miss the animal, and had ended up in a ditch.

The first I knew of it was when the alarm bell rang at the fire station.

"Bus in ditch in Pontypandy Lane," said Station Officer Steele, reading the computer print-out. "*Action stations,* Fireman Sam!"

Hurrying to Jupiter, we drove the big, red fire engine quickly down the hill towards Pontypandy Lane. Trevor was very pleased to see us. He had tried pushing the bus out of the ditch himself.

"I slipped, and fell in a muddy puddle!" he sighed sadly, as we looked at our mud-covered friend.

"You look like you've bathed in it, Trevor," I laughed. "Still, we'll soon have your bus out."

I could see that the bus would be easy to push out. So while Trevor started the engine, Station Officer Steele and I went to the front of the bus.

"One, er, two, three, *push*!" ordered the Station Officer.

The bus slithered and slipped, and then was free!

But before we could catch our breaths, a message came through over Jupiter's radio.

"Fire at Price's General Store!"

"*Great Fires of London*!" I cried, as we all hurried to Jupiter. "Now what's happened?"

"Oh, dear!" groaned Trevor. "I hope my Dilys is all right!"

Dilys was fine, and so was Norman. It was he who had seen the black smoke pouring out of the kitchen window. He had run to the telephone box and dialled 999.

Dilys was happy to hear the "Nee! Nah! Nee! Nah!" of Jupiter's siren as I drove the fire engine quickly into Pontypandy.

"*Man the fire extinguishers*!" ordered Station Officer Steele.

Trevor and I ran into the store. The kitchen was filled with thick, black smoke.

Trevor turned the gas ring off, while I sprayed the pan with foam to make sure the pan wouldn't catch alight.

"Everything's all right now," I said, as we went outside again.

"Except my dinner!" cried Dilys. "Now what am I going to feed Trevor?"

It was then that Dilys saw Trevor covered in mud. And Trevor saw Dilys, her face and hands covered in black ink.

"Ha, ha! What a sight you look, Trevor!" Dilys laughed.

"Ho, ho! What about you, Dilys?" chuckled Trevor.

Trevor gave Dilys a tiny kiss on the cheek. "I don't care what you look like," he said. "You'll always be special to me."

"And you can both join me and the twins for dinner at the fire station," I said.

Trevor and Dilys thought this was a grand idea. And it was the best night out we all had had in ages!

Your friend
Fireman Sam

Moon Monster!

To make your own Moon Monster like mine, you will need: A cotton reel, a rubber band, a candle, a stick about ten centimetres long, a used match, a piece of stiff paper, a pair of round ended scissors, two pipe cleaners and some sticky tape.

Push the rubber band through the cotton reel, and then put the matchstick through the loop at one end of the rubber band. Stick the match down with a piece of sticky tape.

Get a grown-up to carefully cut a slice of candle, about one centimetre in thickness, then make a hole through it with the rounded ended scissors.

Push the free end of the rubber band through the centre of the candle and put the stick through the loop.

Draw a circle on to some thick paper, using a middle-sized plate, and carefully cut it out.

Fold the circle in half and then half again. Unfold the paper and carefully cut along one of the creases to the middle.

Curl the paper around so that it makes a cone, stick the edges together with the sticky tape. Then cut two slits in the cone to make a flap.

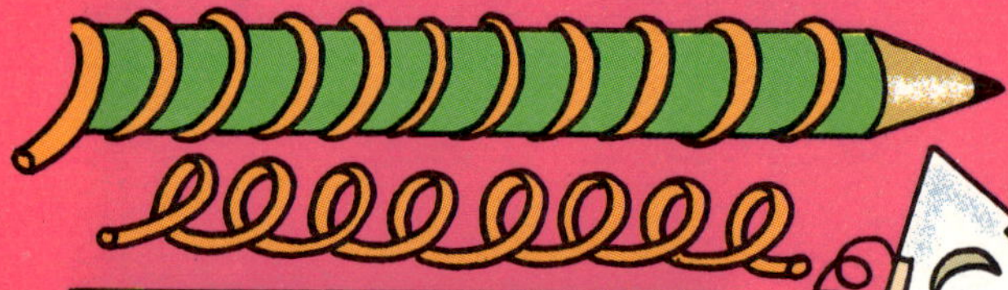

To make some antennae, wind a pipe cleaner round a pencil, then slide it off. Stick it to the cone with the sticky tape. Wind up the cotton reel motor by turning the stick lots of times.

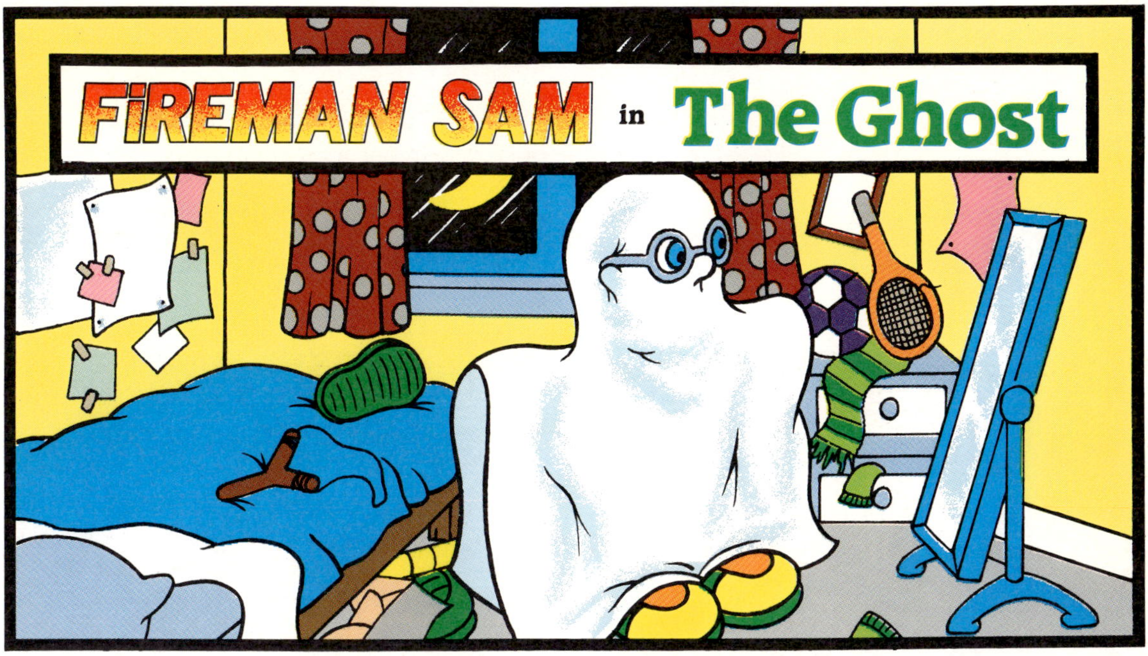

Night had fallen in Pontypandy. Norman Price was in his bedroom at Price's General Store. He was cutting two eye-holes in an old sheet his mum had thrown out.

Norman put the sheet over his head and peeped through the eye-holes. He looked at himself in the mirror. "*Cor! Megabrill!*" he said, "I look just like a *real* ghost!"

Norman silently crept downstairs. Dilys was in the kitchen, whipping some cream in a bowl. Norman sneaked up behind her. "*Booo!*" he cried in an eerie voice.

"*Shriiiieeek!*" screamed Dilys when she saw the 'ghost'. She threw her arms up in fright. The bowl of cream somersaulted in the air and landed on her head!

"*Norman*! Just wait until I get my hands on you. Giving your poor mam such a fright," shouted Dilys. Norman ran out of the store. He was laughing fit to burst!

Elvis Cridlington was walking home from his shift at the fire station. Norman was hiding behind the post-box. When Elvis passed by, Norman jumped out.

"*Aaaggh!* I'm too young to be haunted!" screamed Elvis in alarm. He ran away as fast as he could. "*Heh! Heh!* Now to frighten Bella," laughed Norman.

Bella was just about to close her cafe, when Norman strolled in. "*Mama-mia*! It's-a ghost!" cried Bella. She stumbled back and accidentally hit the fire alarm.

Fireman Sam was working the night shift at the fire station when the alarm came through. He climbed aboard Jupiter and quickly drove over to Bella's cafe.

Sam ran into the cafe, carrying the fire hose. "Rightio, Bella. Where's the fire?" asked Sam. Then he saw the 'ghost'. *"Great Fires of London!"* he cried.

"Don't squirt me, Sam!" wailed Norman, pulling the sheet off. "I'm sorry I played a trick on you all." Then Norman screamed. "There's a real ghost in Bella's garden!"

Norman ran off. Sam looked out of the window. "That's no ghost," he laughed. "It's only Bella's sheets on the washing line. That'll serve Norman right. Ha, ha!"

The End

Missing Map!

Fireman Sam has had a phone call from Bella – her cat, Rosa, is stuck up a tree again! But Sam has lost his map. Can you help him find his way through the maze of country roads?

Party Fun!

Every morning, before Sam goes to work at the Pontypandy Fire Station, he pays a visit to Bella Lasagne's cafe.

"Morning, Bella!" said Sam cheerfully, one bright, sunny morning. "Are my sandwiches ready?"

Bella always made Sam a packed lunch to take to work. Sometimes she would make him his very favourite cheese and pickle sandwiches – sometimes cucumber and tomato ones, and on very cold days, Bella would make pepperoni sandwiches to help keep Sam warm!

"*Mama-mia*! I-a completely forget!" cried Bella, bursting into tears. "My mind, it's-a not on the job today!"

Sam didn't like to see Bella so upset.

"Don't worry, Bella," he said kindly, handing her a clean handkerchief to wipe away her tears. "I can always get Elvis to make me something in the station canteen!"

"*Elvis*?" said Bella, in surprise.

Sam chuckled. "Aye, you're right there. Maybe that's not such a good idea," he chuckled. "Last time Elvis tried boiling an egg, we ended up with yolk all over the ceiling! Perhaps I'd better cook something *myself.*"

Bella gave Sam back his handkerchief.

"I'm-a sorry for being a silly, Sam!" she said. "I love-a living in Pontypandy. I just-a sometimes feel lonely for my home, Italy, where I was born! I can see clearly, the canals, gondolas, the Leaning Tower of-a the Pisa. Aaah, *home*!"

"Great Fires of London!" said Sam. "I know what the problem is! You're homesick, Bella! But don't worry. We'll soon have you smiling again!"

Sam left the cafe and caught Trevor Evans' bus up to the fire station. He told Station Officer Steele about Bella.

"I have a great idea, Sir," said Sam. "Why don't *we* hold a special Italian party for Bella at the station?"

"Jolly good, er, thinking, Fireman Sam!" agreed Station Officer Steele. "Just the, um, thing to lift Mrs Lasagne's spirits! Cridlington can cook up some special Italian food, we can hang up some Italian flags, and the Pontypandy Brass Band can play some favourite old Italian songs!"

Sam spent the morning outside in the station's driveway, hanging up red, white and green bunting and brightly coloured balloons. Elvis was in the kitchen, cooking a large pan of spaghetti.

"Cor! Bit tricky this!" he said, lifting the long strands of spaghetti out of the pan with two large spoons.

"Bloomin' nuisance it is too!" he grumbled, as the spaghetti slithered and slipped between the spoons, then dropped into his boots, and *all over* the floor!

The spaghetti was still quite hot, and burnt Elvis's feet!

"*Ooow! Owch!*" wailed Elvis, hopping around the kitchen, trying to pull his boots off. He stumbled backwards and crashed into the table!

"*Oh, no!*" groaned Elvis, as a bowl of hot, sticky ravioli sauce fell off the table and into his lap with a loud and very messy *sploot!*

Station Officer Steele came into the kitchen to see how the dinner was coming along.

"*Cridlington!* What on earth are you doing?" he spluttered, when he saw the mess.

"Er, just tasting the sauce, like," blushed Elvis, licking the sauce off his fingers. "*Hmmm!* Very tasty. Everything's, er, under control, Sir!"

"Very good, Cridlington!" said the Station Officer, turning to leave. "But don't sit down resting all day. Mrs Lasagne and her friends will be here in a few hours! I want everything shipshape and tickety-boo before they arrive!"

"Aye, aye, Sir!" sighed Elvis.

Bella was just closing the cafe when Sam drove Jupiter into Pontypandy.

"*Bellisima*! What's the trouble, Sam?" she asked him as he parked Jupiter outside her cafe. "My chip pan, she-a not on the fire again, is she?"

"Ha, ha! There's no fire, Bella!" chuckled Sam. "I've come to give you a lift to the fire station. Come on, hop in!"

Bella didn't know what Sam was up to, but she had always wanted a ride in Jupiter. Sam even let her sound the siren to tell everyone they were coming. "*Nee! Nah! Nee! Nah!*" wailed Jupiter.

Sam drove the fire engine up the hill to the fire station. When Bella saw the special Italian decorations around the station, and all her friends waiting to greet her, she burst into tears.

"This is such-a surprise!" she said happily. "It's not-a even my birthday! *Is it*?"

"Ha, ha! Of course it isn't, Bella!" laughed Sam. "I thought you'd like a special Italian party to remind you of your home!"

"Glad to see you, Bella!" said Dilys happily, dragging her by the arm to a table of delicious looking food. "I made you a special cake! It looks just like the *Toppling Tower of Pizzas!*"

Bella laughed. "That's-a the Leaning Tower of Pisa, but it-a no matter! It's-a lovely! Just like-a my mother used to make! Thank you, Mrs Price!" And she gave Dilys a kiss on the cheek.

"So emotional, these Italians!" sighed Dilys, as Bella hugged her.

As the evening went on, Sam turned on the station lights, and the firemen brought out their musical instruments. Station Officer Steele raised his baton, and the Pontypandy Brass Band began to play.

Everyone danced and clapped along in time to the music.

"*Oom-pa-pa! Oom-pa-pa!* Just-a like the music from my Italy!" said Bella, dancing with Norman.

"Crikey! Watch where you're going, Bella!" groaned Norman, as Bella stepped on his foot for the *third* time!

Suddenly, all the lights went out!

"Great Fires of London!" cried Sam. "The fuse has blown, and it's too dark to carry on without lights."

"Oh, dear!" groaned James. "We don't want the party to end. Do *something*, Uncle Sam!"

So Sam did! He got permission from Station Officer Steele to bring Jupiter out of the Appliance Shed. He turned on the fire engine's lights. They lit up the driveway brightly for everyone to see.

"Well done, Fireman Sam!" said Station Officer Steele. "Quick, er, thinking! Now the party can continue!"

And it did, all night long!

"This is the happiest day of my-a life!" said Bella, crying again. "Sometimes I miss-a my Italy, but I'm glad I live in Pontypandy, with my very *best* friends!"

THE END

Pontypandy Panic!

"Help!" cries James as another of Sam's wacky inventions carries him off. Join the dots to find out what Sarah is giggling at!

FiREMAN SAM
The Treasure Map

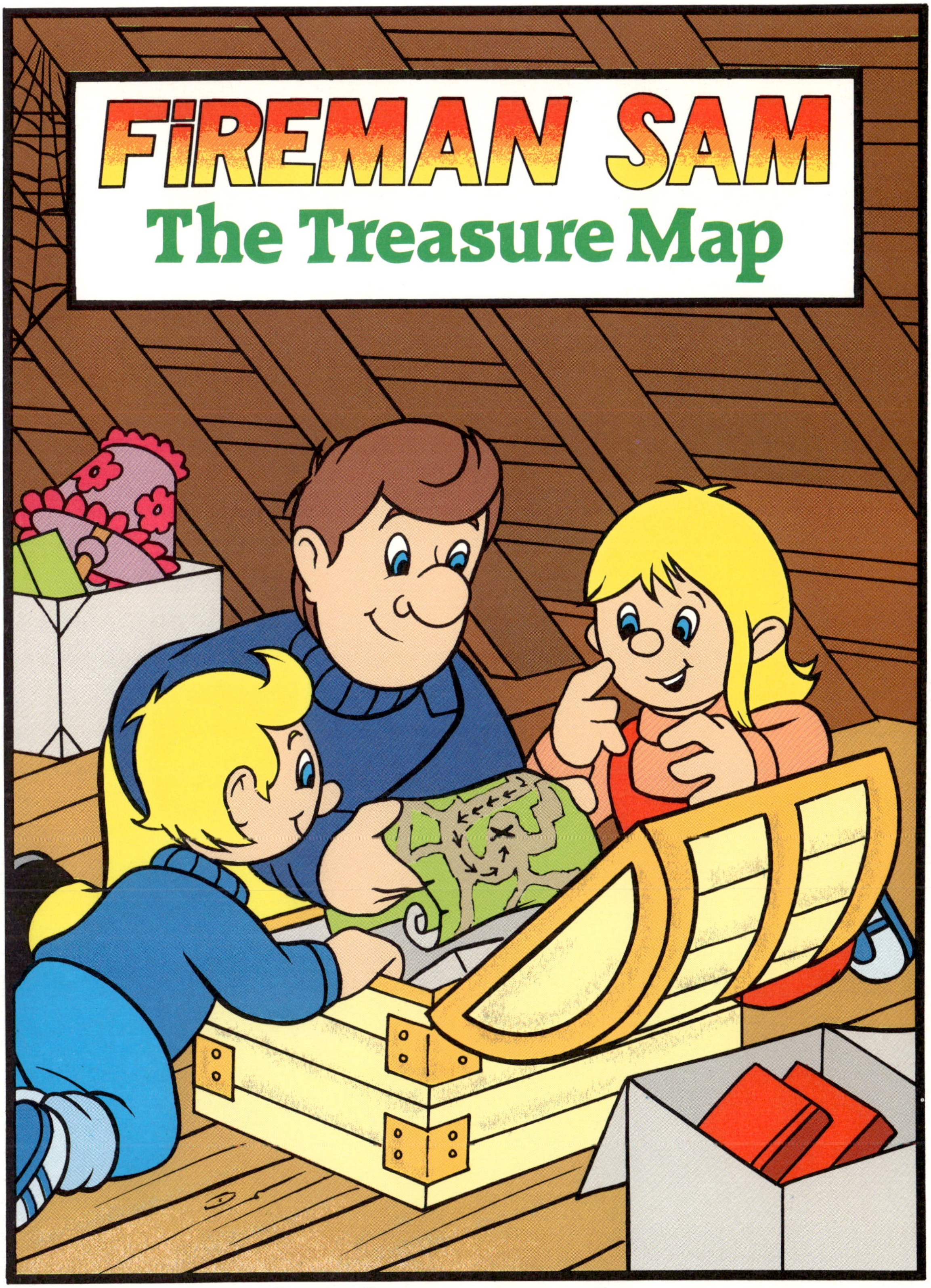

Fireman Sam had been cleaning his attic out. He found a map in an old wooden chest. "It's a treasure map!" shouted Sarah and James, who were helping Sam.

"*Ho, ho*! Treasure map indeed!" laughed Sam, turning to look. "It looks like a map of the Pontypandy Hills to me. But you can have it to play with if you like."

When Sam had gone to work, the children looked at the map. They wanted to be the first to find the treasure! They followed the map to an old cave high up in the hills.

"*Oooh!* It looks really dark!" said Sarah, nervously, peering inside the cave. "Perhaps we shouldn't go any further?" "Don't be such a scaredy cat," laughed James.

So both children went deep into the cave. In the dark, it was really hard to tell where they were going. Suddenly, James tripped and fell down a deep, dark hole!

Luckily, he wasn't hurt. But the hole *was* very deep and James couldn't climb out. "Don't worry, James," cried Sarah, peering down at him. "I'll fetch Uncle Sam."

Sarah carefully felt her way out of the cave and ran quickly to a nearby telephone box. She picked up the receiver and dialled 999 and asked for the fire service.

Sam was in the Crew Room when the alarm came through. "Boy trapped down hole in cave," said Station Officer Steele, reading the message from the teleprinter.

"*Great Fires of London*!" gasped Sam in alarm. He ran over to the fireman's pole, and slid quickly down to the Appliance Room. Elvis had already started Jupiter.

Elvis quickly drove Jupiter out of the fire station. Sam put the siren on to let everyone know they were on their way. "*Nee! Nah! Nee! Nah!*" it wailed noisily.

Sarah was waiting patiently for the firemen outside the cave. "Rightio, Elvis," said Sam. "Bring the rope and the safety harness. We'll need them to rescue James!"

Sam put the safety harness on and tied the rope to it. Elvis wrapped the rest of the rope around his waist. Then Sam lowered himself down the hole.

James was really relieved to see his uncle. Sam put the safety harness around James. "Rightio, Elvis," he called. "Pull him up." Elvis pulled James out of the hole.

When James was safely up, he then pulled Sam up. "Next time, try exploring my attic," Sam said. "There's a special treasure chest there – full of my old toys!" he laughed.

The End

Mystic Messages!

Sam has got a special treat in store for Sarah and James. Sarah has written a secret message to James telling him what it is, so that no one else will find out. Help James to read what it says.

Speedy Steele!

Oh no! Elvis has set the fire station on fire again! Help Station Officer Steele get to the station to put out the fire. All you need is a dice and some coloured counters. The first person to throw a six starts.

31
30
29
8
26
32
33
34
35
36
37
38
39
40
41
42
43
44
45
46
47
48
49
50
51
52
53
54
55
56
57
58
You find a secret path. Take it!
A water pipe has burst. You stop to repair it. Go back six places.
Naughty Norman has changed the sign post. Go back ten places.
Fire Station
Well done! But you needn't have worried. It was only Elvis's breakfast going up in smoke and not the fire station!

Bath-Time!

Fireman Sam was busy in his inventing shed.

"Now the doo-wotzit goes to the calibrator and that ties to the toggle-switch, like *so*!" said Sam, hammering away at his latest invention.

Sarah and James had come to visit Sam. They were waiting impatiently outside the shed for him to finish.

"*Hurry up*, Uncle Sam!" called James. "You said you'd be finished *ages* ago!"

"Nearly done!" said Sam, over the sounds of even more crashes, bangs and wallops!

"What are you making anyway?" asked Sarah, trying to peer inside the shed through a knothole in the door, without much success.

"Never you mind!" laughed Sam. "All I'll say is that it's my best invention *yet*!"

"I don't like the sound of that!" giggled James. "Uncle Sam's inventions *always* go wrong!"

"Rightio! All done!" said Sam, coming out of the shed, cleaning his hands with an oily rag.

Sam was dressed in his fireman's uniform. He was working at the Pontypandy Fire Station later that day.

"Oooh! Please let us see it, Uncle Sam!" begged James.

"Oooh! Yes! Please! Please! *Please*!" shouted Sarah, hopping about, excitedly.

"Aye, well, someone's got to be the first, and it may as well be you two!" chuckled Sam.

He went back inside the inventing shed. The twins could hear more crashes and bangs, before Sam came out wheeling a bath in front of him.

The children were very disappointed!

"Aww, is that *all*?" groaned James. "I thought it was something special! We've got one of those at home! It's a *torture device*!"

Sam chuckled. "Cheeky! You wouldn't half pong if we didn't all have baths! Anyway, this one's different!"

"*How*?" asked Sarah.

"This is a multi-directional, do-it-for-yourself bath!" said Sam, proudly. "It will wash your face, shampoo your hair, scrub your back, clean your ears and polish your feet all at the same time, while singing, 'I'm For Ever Blowing Bubbles'!"

"*Coo*!" said the twins together.

"Clever, eh?" said Sam. "Mind you, there's still one or two little things that need fixing before it's properly operational!"

"But why's it on wheels?" asked James.

"So you can take it with you on holiday, *of course*!" said Sam. "There's a water tank inside so you don't even have to fix it to a water pipe. You can enjoy a nice, relaxing bath *whenever* you feel like it!"

"*Mega-brill*!" said Sarah. "I can't wait to try it out! Show us how it works, Uncle Sam!"

Sam pressed a button on the side of the bath. A mechanical arm reached out and pushed the plug into the plug-hole. Then the taps began to run water into the bath.

"Then all you do is press this button," said Sam, pointing to a second button, "to set the rest of the machinery into action."

James leaned forward for a closer look. "Which? *This* one?" he said, pressing the button.

"*Great Fires of London*! Don't!" shouted Sam. "I told you, it's not *completely* ready yet!"

Too late! The bath began to shake and rumble! *Ch-Chung! Ch-Chung! Ch-Chung*!

"*Oooh*! Should it do that?" asked Sarah, stepping back in case the bath exploded.

"I'm not too sure," said Sam, scratching his head and looking puzzled.

Sam was about to turn the bath off when two pairs of mechanical hands appeared from the sides of the bath, and pulled him in!

The arms began to give Sam, who still had all his clothes on, a bath!

"Ha, ha! Uncle Sam! You do look funny!" giggled Sarah, as Sam's head was suddenly covered in bubbly shampoo. A mechanical arm then began to wash his hair!

Another arm scrubbed Sam's feet while another poured an enormous packet of bubble bath into the water. Soon, there were soap bubbles *everywhere!*

"Now look," said Sam, struggling to stand up. "*Stop washing me,* you mechanical monster!"

The bath was still shaking. This started it rolling on its wheels! It rolled out of Sam's garden through the open gate, and down the street towards Pontypandy!

"*Great Fires of London*!" groaned Sam, as the villagers looked on in amazement. "Will someone please stop this thing and help me?"

"Oh, my goodness! Look out, Norman!" said Dilys, as she watched the bath rolling towards her shop. "What will that Sam get up to next?"

"*Mama-mia*!" gasped Bella in alarm. "Is that-a Sam's new motor car?"

Sam was still struggling to get out of the bath. A mechanical hand suddenly pulled off one of his boots.

"*Whoops*!" said Sam, as he slipped down the bath in his wet clothes. His foot slid forwards, and Sam's big toe got caught in the tap!

Luckily, the bath ran gently into a tree and stopped. Sam reached over, and pressed the button to turn the machine off.

"Phew! I'm glad that's over!" said Sam, trying to get out of the bath. But his toe was well and truly stuck!

"Don't worry, Uncle Sam!" said James. "We'll call the fire service!"

D*riiiiiinnnnnnnnnnng!* went the alarm at the fire station.

Station Officer Steele read the report coming through on the teleprinter.

"Fireman Sam trapped in bath with toe stuck in tap!" he read. "*Gracious! This is an emergency*! Come on, Evans!"

Station Officer Steele and Auxiliary Fireman Trevor Evans hurried to Jupiter, the big, red fire engine.

Trevor drove Jupiter quickly down the hill towards Pontypandy. Station Officer Steele set off the siren. *"Nee! Nah! Nee! Nah!"*

Sam was very glad to see his friends coming, though he did feel a little silly!

"Right, Fireman Sam!" said Station Officer Steele. "Soon have you, um, out of there! Evans, fetch the, er, spanner!"

Trevor brought the large spanner from Jupiter's special compartment. Station Officer Steele unscrewed the tap from the bath. Then he squirted oil up the tap.

"One, two, er, three, *pull*!" he said, pulling on the tap. At last, *pop*! Sam's toe was free!

"Thank you, Sir," said Sam, stepping out of the bath, soaking wet! "I think I'll forget about mechanical baths in the future! I'll stick with ordinary ones from now on. They're a *lot* cleaner and safer! *Ha, ha, ha*!"

THE END

Puzzled Price!

Dilys has lots of different things to sell in her shop. In fact, she has so many things that she doesn't really know what she has got! See if you can help her by counting the objects and filling in the answers in the box below. Then see if you can spot the ten mice hidden somewhere in this picture!

How many of the following can you see?

Apples__________
Potatoes__________
Lollipops__________
Jars of jam__________
Oranges__________
Sticks of rock__________
Bottles of lemonade__________
Saucepans__________
Cabbages__________
Floor mops__________
Onions__________
Tins of soup__________
Buckets__________
Spades__________

What number do you get if you add up all the above?____

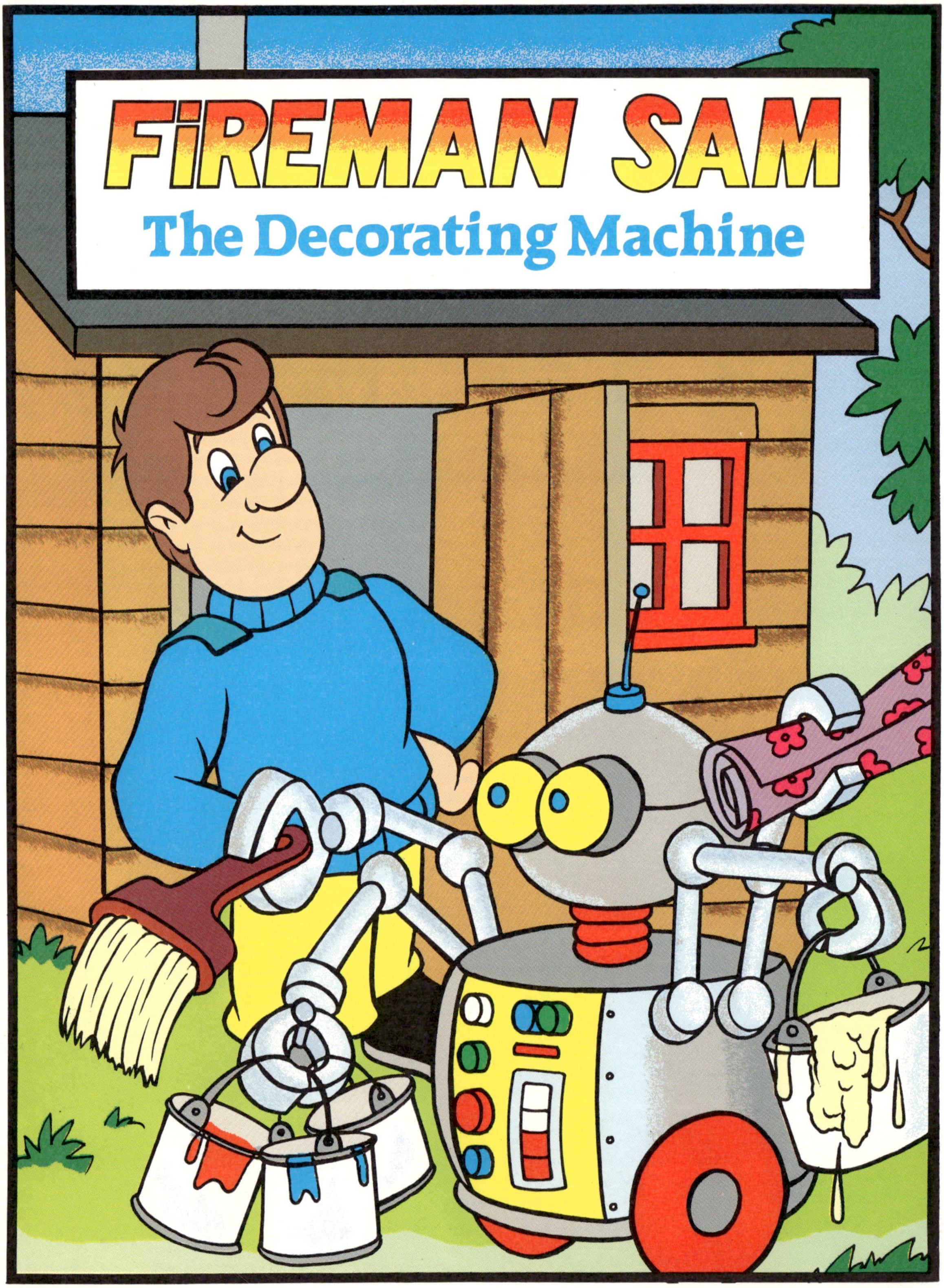

Fireman Sam had decided to re-decorate his house. "Mind you, I don't fancy all that painting, pasting and wall-papering," he thought. "Too much like *hard* work!"

So Sam went over to his special shed. He had decided to invent a decorating machine that would do the job for him. He worked really hard until it was finished.

Sam wanted to try the machine out straight away. But he was on call at the fire station. "I'll leave it in the garden until I get back," he said as he walked off to work.

But then, Dilys Price came into Sam's garden with his groceries. She was surprised to see the decorating machine. "What's our Sam up to now?" she wondered.

But unluckily, Dilys thought it was a tea-making machine! "*Oh*! I could just do with a cuppa!" she said, pressing one of the buttons. The machine's eyes lit up.

"*Paint! Paste! Re-decorate*!" the machine said. Its arms moved up and down waving paintbrushes to and fro. *Splaaat!* The machine painted Dily's face a bright red.

"*Ooooh! Help!* It's gone bloomin' bonkers!" cried Dilys. She ran out of Sam's garden. The decorating machine followed behind. It chased Dilys all around Pontypandy.

The machine wallpapered Trevor's bus. Then it pasted Bella's face. "*Mama-mia*!" cried Bella, running back inside her cafe. "It is-a monster from space!"

Before long, everything in Pontypandy had been painted, pasted or wallpapered! Even Rosa, Bella's cat. "*Help*!" cried Dilys, who was still being chased.

Fireman Sam was driving Jupiter into Pontypandy. He had taken the fire engine out to test the new brake pads. "*Goodness*!" he gasped, when he saw the mess.

Sam stopped Jupiter. He fetched the hose and turned it on. Water squirted from the hose and knocked the machine over before it could do any more harm.

Dilys ran over to Sam and gave him a big kiss. "You saved me, Sam!" she smiled. Then she told him off for leaving the machine in the garden in the first place.

Sam looked at the mess his machine had made in Pontypandy. "I've never seen blue trees or papered postboxes before!" he said. He did feel really silly!

No one really minded and Sam promised to clean up Pontypandy before he went home. "We must have the most colourful village in the world!" laughed Trevor.

The End

Ponty Puppet

It was raining really hard in Pontypandy one day, and Sarah was bored. So to cheer herself up, she decided to make a puppet of her favourite uncle, Fireman Sam. If you would like to make one too, then why not follow Sarah's easy instructions?

To make your very own Fireman Sam puppet, you will need:
Some tracing paper
A piece of thin card
Some crayons, pens, paints or pencils
A pair of round-ended scissors
Four paper fasteners
A lollipop stick
Some sticky tape

1. Trace the arms and legs on the opposite page on to some thin card. Then, colour all the pieces in. Carefully cut them out and make holes in the card where indicated – a hole puncher is best for doing this.

2. Fix the arms and legs to the body using the paper fasteners. Make sure that each part can move easily. Now, stick the lollipop stick to the back of the body.

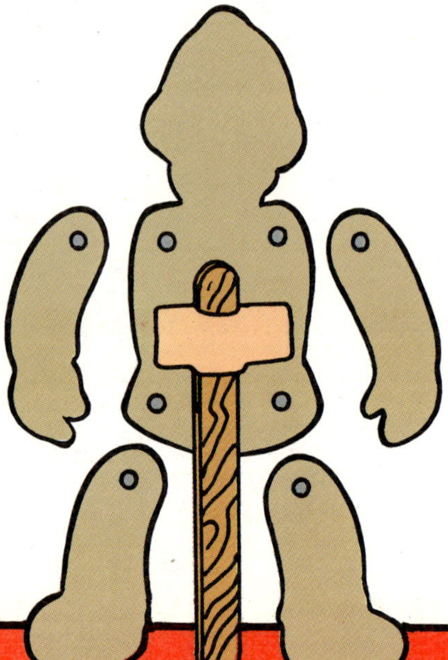

Shake the stick up and down and from side to side, and watch Fireman Sam perform his crazy, hip hop dance.

Right Leg

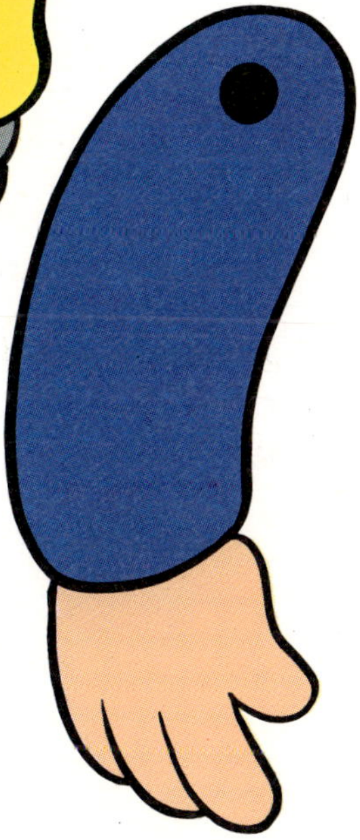

Right Arm

Body

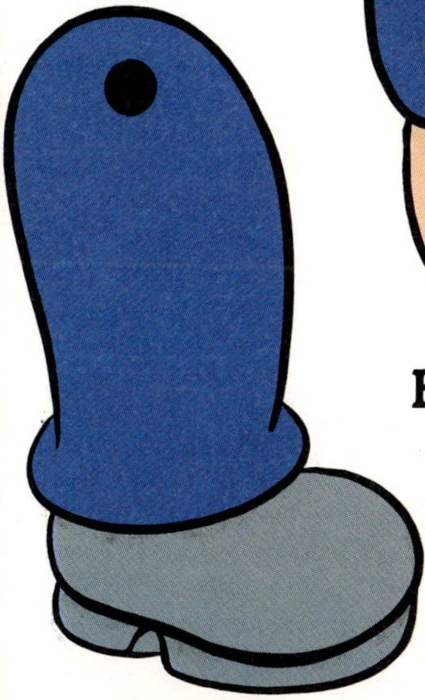

Left Leg

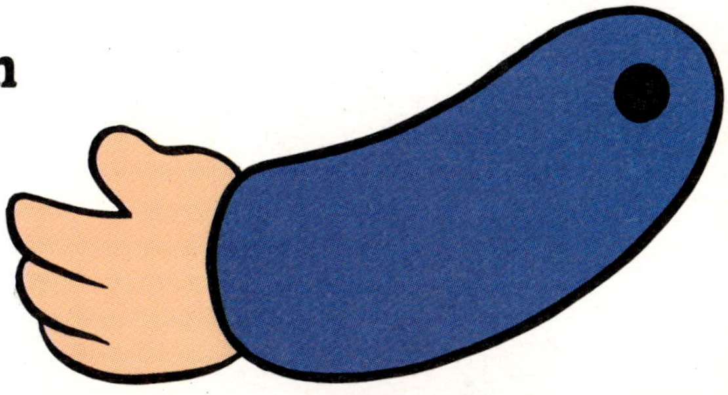

Left Arm

The Medal!

Station Officer Steele was very proud of his long-service medal.

"I was, um, presented with it for my, er, twenty-five years as a fireman," he told Norman Price one day.

"*Cor!* It's *mega-brill!*" said Norman, holding the medal in his hand. "I'm going to be a fireman too, when I grow up. Then I'll get a medal *as well!*"

Norman had come to the Pontypandy Fire Station to earn some extra pocket money. Station Officer Steele had agreed to let him wash Jupiter, the big, red fire engine.

"But you *mustn't* get in the way, young Price," said the Station Officer. "A fire station is a *very* busy place, and I have to get ready to go to Newtown. I have an important talk to give on fire safety at the Town Hall this evening."

"You won't even know I'm here," said Norman. "Scouts honour!"

"You're *not* in the Scouts, Norman!" said Trevor Evans, laughing.

"Oh, yeah!" said Norman slyly. "I completely forgot!"

Norman fetched the hose from the Appliance Shed. Elvis Cridlington had already driven Jupiter out of it, and had parked it in the driveway, all ready to be washed.

Norman started to spray Jupiter with water from the hose. Then, for a laugh, he sprayed Elvis too!

"Hmmm! *Very funny!*" said Elvis, squelching back into the station, dripping wet.

Station Officer Steele had decided he would wear his special medal when he gave the talk at the Town Hall.

"It will add an air of, um, dignity, to my uniform!" he decided, as he brushed his fireman's jacket clean.

Fireman Sam had just arrived at the station to take over Watch Duty from Elvis.

"Very smart you look too, Sir," he said. "Mind you, your helmet could do with a good polish."

"Quite, er, right, Fireman Sam," said Station Officer Steele. "Well spotted! I shall clean it straight away!"

After Station Officer Steele had gone to fetch the polish, and Sam had left for the Crew Room, Norman Price entered the room.

"All finished!" he said. "*Pay up!*"

He was disappointed to find that no one was waiting for him. Then he saw the long-service medal on the table.

"*Wow*! I'll just borrow this for a few hours! Then I can play at being a *real* fireman!" he said. "I'll have it back before anyone notices it's gone!"

Norman took the medal and pinned it to his jumper. Then he ran out of the station, and hurried down the hill towards Pontypandy.

"*Nee! Nah! Nee! Nah!* Station Officer Price hurries to save Pontypandy from the great fire!" he shouted, pretending to drive Jupiter quickly between some tricky lamp posts!

Norman was so busy playing, he didn't see Bella Lasagne's cat, Rosa, until he tripped over her.

"You *silly* moggy!" cried Norman, tumbling to the ground. As Norman hit the pavement, the long-service medal fell off his jumper, and dropped through the grating of a drain.

"Lummy! Now what am I going to do?" groaned Norman. "Station Officer Steele is going to go *potty* about this!"

Station Officer Steele was already feeling quite upset!

"Dear me! Now where did *I put it*?" he muttered, searching around his desk and on the floor for the medal. "I know it *was here* this morning!"

"Well, it can't just have vanished into thin air," said Sam. "We'll search the whole station. It's *bound* to turn up!"

But the medal was nowhere to be found.

"Perhaps it got put into the kitchen cupboard," said Elvis Cridlington, opening the cupboard door.

Crraaasssh! Pots and pans tumbled out, bouncing off Elvis's head.

"*Oooow!*" he shouted, stepping back and getting his foot caught in one of the pots.

"*Cridlington! You've put your foot in it again!*" shouted Station Officer Steele, as Sam pulled hard on the pot to free Elvis.

The pot came off, and Elvis stumbled backwards, to land on his bottom with a good hard *bump!*

"This is no good *at all*!" sighed Station Officer Steele sadly. "My medal is lost! I shall have to attend the Town Hall without it."

It was then that the fire alarm rang. Trevor Evans came running in.

"Medal dropped down drain in Pontypandy!" he said breathlessly.

"*Great Fires of London!*" said Sam. "The long-service medal! It has *to be!*"

Sam, Trevor and Steele hurried to Jupiter.

They climbed into the cab, and Sam set off the engine's siren to let people know they were on their way. "*Nee! Nah! Nee! Nah!*"

Norman was waiting for them beside the drain.

"I'm *really* sorry I took your medal," said Norman sheepishly, as Station Officer Steele got out of Jupiter. "I only wanted it to play with!"

"No time for that now, Price lad!" said the Station Officer sternly. "*Action Stations,* men. Fireman Cridlington, *lift* the drain grating. Fireman Sam, *retrieve* the medal!"

Once the grating was out of the way, Sam lay down on the road, and reached into the drain with his hand.

"I can't quite reach it, Sir," he said, standing up again. "My arm's *not* long enough."

"What can *we do*?" sighed Station Officer Steele, feeling very upset. "That medal means a *great* deal to me!"

Sam went over to Jupiter. He came back with a coat-hanger from one of Jupiter's compartments.

"Don't worry, Sir," he said, straightening out the coat-hanger. "I'll soon get it back for you."

Sam twisted one end of the coat-hanger into a hook. Then he lowered it down the drain. He caught the medal ribbon on the hook, and pulled it back up.

"*Bravo,* Fireman Sam! Jolly good idea!" said Station Officer Steele, beaming. He pinned the medal to his uniform.

"And *never* take things that don't belong to you, Norman," said Sam. "*Always ask first.*"

"I will, Sam!" said Norman. "*I promise!*"

"Rightio," grinned Sam. "And to make up for all the trouble you caused, you can sweep out the station, *free of charge*!"

"*Aww, Sam!*" groaned Norman.

"Quite right too, Fireman Sam!" agreed Station Officer Steele. "This will teach young Price to *clean up* his act! Ha, ha! Little joke there, what!"

THE END

Mad Machines!

Oh dear! Sam's tidy-up machine has got carried away. It's trying to tell Trevor Evans who the objects belong to, but Trevor doesn't understand. Can you help him by sorting out the names and putting them to the right objects?

Trevor Evans is a part-time fireman. When he isn't working at the station, he's driving his bus. One sunny day, he stopped his bus on top of a hill beside a grassy field.

Trevor went into the field to have a little rest. He sat down, and was soon fast asleep! Norman Price was also in the field. He was looking for lots of slugs and worms.

"I don't fancy walking home," he said glumly. Then he saw Trevor and his bus. "*Mega-brill*!" he said to himself. "I'll hide on the bus and get a free ride home. *Yeah*!"

Norman sneaked aboard the bus but accidentally hit the handbrake, releasing it. The bus started to roll down the hill. "*Waaaah*!" cried Norman, feeling very scared.

Luckily, the bus rolled to a stop in a duck pond. The noise woke Trevor up. He was glad to see Norman wasn't hurt. But his bus was stuck in the pond.

Trevor called the fire brigade on his two-way radio. Fireman Sam took the call and then drove Jupiter quickly over to the pond. "Rightio, Trevor," said Sam.

Sam tied a rope from Jupiter to the bus. Then he slowly drove Jupiter forward, and pulled the bus out of the pond. The bus was completely covered in mud.

"Now, Norman lad," laughed Sam. "You can clean this bus, to make up for all the trouble you caused." Norman grumbled. "*Yeugh*! Next time, I'm going to walk!"

The End

Naughty Norman!

Norman Price is always up to sort of mischief. Here is his favourite trick to try on your friends and family!

Only play tricks on people with a sense of humour!

Get a sheet of blotting paper and place it on to some old newspapers. Now, very carefully, pour a very small amount of ink on to the blotting paper. After at least an hour, when the ink has completely dried, cut around the shapes the ink has made.

Then place the ink blots beside an empty ink pot, so that it looks as though an accident has happened! Then ask your victim in to look at the mess you've made. Stand back and watch their reaction – from a safe distance of course!

A Report!

Hello, readers!

It was a hot, sunny day in Pontypandy. There I was, in my inventing shed, wondering what fabulous thing to invent next, when there came a loud scream from Price's General Store.

"*Eeeeeeeeeeeeeek!*"

"*Great Fires of London!*" I cried, running out of the garden. "It sounds as if the whole of Pontypandy's on fire!"

Daft of me to think that really. It's not as if there were any flames or anything!

When I reached the Store, a bit out of breath (I'd just eaten a big breakfast!), Dilys was standing outside, jiggling up and down.

"Is that a new dance craze, Dilys?" I asked, trying not to laugh.

"Glad to see you, Sam!" said Dilys. "Please help! A *monster's* trying to eat me!"

"M*onster*?" I said, looking around. I was expecting to see a three-headed fire breathing dragon or something. "There's no monster here, Dilys!"

"*There is too!*" said Dilys, pointing to a large black spider on the back of her dress. "My Norman saw it, just a minute ago! He's such a *brave* boy, my Norman! Mummy's little darling!"

I looked closely at the spider and burst out laughing!

"He's also a good practical joker," I said, picking the spider off her dress. "This is a *fake* spider, see? It's made of *plastic!*"

"*Ooooh!* Wait until I get my hands on him!" shouted Dilys, running back inside the shop. "I'll give him what for!"

She came back, dragging Norman by his very red ear!

"Leave off, Mam!" groaned Norman. "It was only a joke. I was bored! There's nothing to do here!"

It was then that Sarah and James appeared. They had heard the noise and had come to see what was happening.

"Why don't you play with us, Norman?" said James cheerfully. "We're going to play pirates in the park."

"*Cor! Mega-brill!*" cried Norman, smiling. "I bagsy being Cap'n Black Jake, terror of the Seven Seas! Avast there me hearties! Let's go and search for buried treasure in Davey Jones' Locker! Oooh! Arrr!"

But quite quickly, yes, you guessed it, Norman got bored again!

"Aww, this is *rubbish!*" he grumbled, after they had all been playing for only ten minutes. "Real pirates have real ships to sail on."

"Don't talk wet, Norman," said Sarah crossly. "Where are we going to find a proper ship in the park!"

"Why don't we *build* one," he said. "Or, at least, we can build a raft! My Mam's got lots of planks of wood behind her store. *Come on!*"

The children fetched the planks. They worked really hard roping them all together until they had made themselves a raft.

"Now, let's take it to the park pond," said Norman, excitedly.

James wasn't so sure. "Uncle Sam has warned us not to play near water," he said. "In case we fall in."

"Don't be such a *scaredy-cat!*" grumbled Norman. "The pond's not deep, and we'll tie some rope from the raft to a tree. That way we'll be safe!"

Norman's a sensible lad, most of the time. It's a pity none of his ideas *ever* work!

The children were soon playing pirates on the raft in the pond.

"Ha, ha! Two against one! You'll never make Black Jake walk the plank!" cackled Norman.

He bounced up and down on the raft, swinging a stick that he was pretending was a sword.

All this bouncing around made the raft rock from side to side. It also pulled the rope loose from the tree. The raft drifted quickly and silently away from the edge of the pond.

"*Yipes!* We're sailing!" cried Sarah, as the raft splashed towards the middle of the pond. "We'll never reach the path from here. *We're stuck!*"

"Hellllllllp!" they all shouted together.

Luckily Trevor Evans was passing by the park in his bus. He saw the children trapped on the raft.

"This is a job for the fire service!" he said. He stopped his bus and ran to the nearest telephone box and dialled 999.

I was on Watch Duty at the Pontypandy Fire Station. I was checking Jupiter's compartments to make sure all the fire-fighting equipment was put away properly.

Drrrriiiinnnnnnnng went the alarm on the station wall.

Station Officer Steele was in the Crew Room. He read the message from the tele-printer. "Children trapped on raft in park! Right, men! *Action stations!"* he cried.

Elvis Cridlington slid down the fire pole, instantly followed by Station Officer Steele.

By this time I had started up Jupiter.

Before you could say, "Three leeks for a Welshman!" we were driving quickly towards Pontypandy.

"*Nee! Nah! Nee! Nah!*" wailed Jupiter's siren.

I drove Jupiter into the park and stopped at the pond.

"Don't worry, kids!" I shouted to the children. "We'll soon have you shipshape and safe back on dry land again!"

Elvis fetched the rope from Jupiter. I tied my helmet to one end of the rope to make it heavy, and then I threw the rope carefully towards the edge of the raft.

Splassssh! The rope landed right next to the raft. Sarah lifted it out of the water. Then all the children held on to it tightly.

Station Officer Steele, Elvis and I pulled the raft back to the edge of the pond.

"*Hurray!* Thanks for rescuing us, Uncle Sam!" said James, as the children climbed on to the path.

"Another job well done!" agreed Station Officer Steele. "And *no one* got wet."

I looked at the raft. "Aye! Good job you made there, kids," I said. "I haven't played pirates for years and years!"

I jumped on to the raft. "Ahoy there, me hearties! I be Pirate Sam!" I shouted. *"Whoops!"*

It was then that the raft tipped over with my heavy weight. I knew I'd had one too many sausages for breakfast! I fell into the pond with a loud *splassssssh!*

Luckily the pond was only fifteen centimetres deep. So there I was, sitting in the water, with a lily pad stuck to my head. How everyone laughed!

"No one got wet but you, Uncle Sam!" giggled Sarah and James.

Your friend
Fireman Sam

Crafty Cats!

Fireman Sam has rushed to rescue ten cats which are stuck up a tree. When he got there though, he could only see one of the ten. Can you help him to spot the other nine?

Fireman Sam arrived early at the Fire Station one day. He wanted to show Steele and Elvis his new invention. "*Hover-boots*!" he laughed, holding them up.

"The hover-boots can fly up and down," explained Sam. "It will save firemen the bother of using ladders." Station Officer Steele thought this was very clever.

"Jolly good, eh what, Fireman Sam? First class," he said. Elvis liked the hover-boots too. "*Cor*! Megabrill! Let's have first try, Sam," he said, putting them on.

"Press this button to go up, Elvis," said Sam. *Whooooosh*! Air suddenly blew out from the bottom of the boots. Elvis rose quickly and gently in the air! "Wow! Fantastic! Sam!"

"*Wow*! This is brill!" shouted Elvis, looking down at Sam and Station Officer Steele. "Press the other button to land," Sam told Elvis, who was looking into the valleys.

Elvis pressed the button, but nothing happened! "*Great Fires of London*!" cried Sam. "Elvis is stuck up there!" Elvis wasn't very happy. "I feel *airsick*!" he said.

Sam fetched a ladder and rested it against the wall. "*Action stations,* Fireman Sam!" said Station Officer Steele. Sam climbed up the ladder to rescue Elvis.

He caught hold of Elvis's feet, and pulled him safely down. "*Oh dear,*" said Sam, throwing the hover-boots away. "I think we'll stick with ladders, after all!"

The End

Puzzle No-More!

Answers to pages 10 & 11:

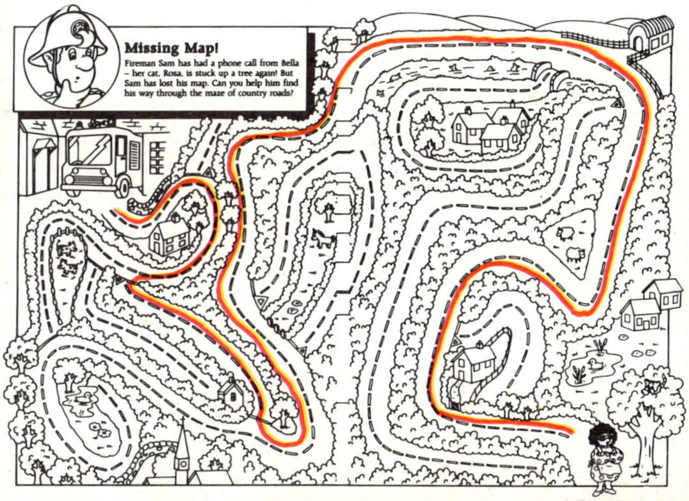

Answers to pages 20 & 21:

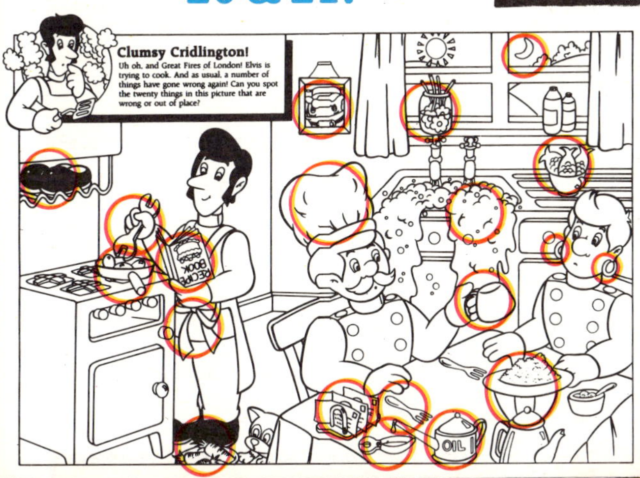

Answer to page 31:

SARAH'S SECRET MESSAGE WAS:
'DEAR JAMES. CAN YOU COME TO THE FIRE STATION AT TWO O'CLOCK ON SUNDAY? WE CAN GO FOR A RIDE IN JUPITER, AND EAT TEA AND CAKE. IT WILL BE FUN. SEE YOU SOON, LOVE SARAH.'

Answers to pages 38 & 39:

Mrs Price had: 11 apples, 8 potatoes, 3 lollipops, 6 jars of jam, 5 oranges, 7 sticks of rock, 4 saucepans, 1 cabbage, 3 floor mops, 9 onions, 3 tins of soup, 3 buckets and 2 spades. Making a grand total of 65 items.

Answer to page 50:

The driver's cap belongs to Trevor Evans, the station report belongs to Station Officer Steele, the glasses belong to Bella Lasagne, the rollers belong to Mrs Price, the chef's hat belongs to Elvis Cridlington and the skateboard belongs to Norman Price.

Answer to page 58:

Meet the folks of Pontypandy!
Sarah and James